P *is for* PHILADELPHIA

P *is for* PHILADELPHIA

SUSAN KORMAN

TEMPLE UNIVERSITY PRESS

Philadelphia

Temple University Press
1601 North Broad Street
Philadelphia PA 19122
www.temple.edu/tempress

Published 2005
Printed in Canada

Design by Andrea Hemmann/GHI Design, Philadelphia
Alphabet illustration by Gina Triplett
Drawings by children of the Philadelphia School District

This book is printed on acid-free paper for greater longevity

Library of Congress Cataloging-in-Publication Data

Korman, Susan.
P is for Philadelphia / Susan Korman. p. cm.
ISBN 1-59213-107-7 (cloth : alk. paper)
1. Philadelphia (Pa.)—Juvenile literature.
2. Philadelphia (Pa.)—History—Juvenile literature.
3. Philadelphia (Pa.)—Social life and customs—Juvenile
literature. 4. English language—Alphabet—Juvenile
literature. I. Title.

F158.33.K67 2005
974.8'11—dc22
2004055331

2 4 6 8 9 7 5 3 1

ACKNOWLEDGMENTS

Temple University Press gratefully acknowledges the support of the
following in underwriting the development and publication of
this book:

BARNES & NOBLE COLLEGE BOOKSTORES

GENO'S

KENTUCKY FRIED CHICKEN

PNC BANK

SODEXHO CAMPUS SERVICES

THE STAPLES FOUNDATION FOR LEARNING

TAWS

TIERNEY COMMUNICATIONS

Temple University Press also gratefully acknowledges the support
of the following institutional collaborators:

THE CITY OF PHILADELPHIA, *Office of the Mayor, Philadelphia Reads*

THE SCHOOL DISTRICT OF PHILADELPHIA, *Office of Creative and Performing Arts*

A is for ATHLETICS...

In Philadelphia, sports fans root for their home teams all year long. Philadelphia is one of just a few cities with teams in all four major-league sports: the Eagles (football), the Flyers (hockey), the 76ers (basketball), and the Phillies (baseball).

In fact, professional baseball was born in Philadelphia in 1865, when the Philadelphia Athletics became the first team to pay a player. Second baseman Alfred J. Reach was paid what was then a big salary—twenty-five dollars per week!

Philadelphia also has several minor-league teams: the Wings (indoor lacrosse), the Phantoms (hockey), and the Kixx (indoor soccer). College sports draw big crowds too, especially when the city hosts the annual Army-Navy football game or when there is a home game for one of the Big 5 basketball teams: Temple University, Villanova University, the University of Pennsylvania (Penn), St. Joseph's University, and La Salle University.

Spring in Philadelphia brings two more exciting events: the Penn Relays, an amateur track meet, and the Dad Vail Regatta, one of the largest college rowing competitions in the country. Each June, at the Pro Cycling Championships, bicyclists race along a hilly course that runs for more than 150 miles. In September, runners compete in the Philadelphia Distance Run, a half-marathon that winds its way through downtown Philadelphia and Fairmount Park.

is for
BENJAMIN FRANKLIN...

Benjamin Franklin is Philadelphia's most famous citizen. Born in Boston, Franklin came to Philadelphia when he was seventeen years old. He left Boston to escape working in his bossy older brother's print shop.

In Philadelphia, Franklin began publishing a newspaper and his popular *Poor Richard's Almanack*. He also became deeply involved in politics. In 1776 he played a key role in the drafting and signing of the Declaration of Independence. At the Constitutional Convention in 1787, he signed the U.S. Constitution. Even in these serious meetings, Franklin never lost his sense of humor. Instead, he liked to try to trip the other delegates as they made their way up the aisle of the Pennsylvania State House!

Franklin is probably best known as a gifted scientist and inventor. (Philadelphia's Franklin Institute Science Museum is named for him.) During his lifetime, Franklin invented many useful devices, including bifocal glasses, the lightning rod, and a new type of clean-burning stove. He was also the brains behind the country's first volunteer fire company, hospital, and library.

When he died in 1790, people of many different religious faiths followed his casket. This was a tribute to the man who had believed so firmly in religious freedom for everyone. Benjamin Franklin is buried at Philadelphia's Christ Church Burial Ground on Arch Street.

C *is for* CHEESE STEAKS...

What do people like to eat in Philadelphia? For one thing, they like to eat cheese steaks—a tasty sandwich piled with sliced beef, onions, and melted cheese.

According to many people, the cheese steak was born in 1930, at Pat's King of Steaks, a restaurant in South Philadelphia (South Philly). Pat's, which is still run by the same family, continues to serve cheese steaks today. Across the street is another famous cheese steak restaurant: Geno's Steaks. Most Philadelphians have strong opinions about which restaurant makes better cheese steaks—Pat's or Geno's!

Other Philadelphia food favorites include hoagies (deli sandwiches made with meat and cheese), soft pretzels, water ice, cinnamon sticky buns, and scrapple. Scrapple was first made by Dutch settlers using cornmeal, seasonings, and boiled pig scraps. Today it is often served with eggs at breakfast time.

Philadelphia food lovers also flock to South Philly's Italian Market for spices, fruits and vegetables, homemade pasta, and cheese. Another popular spot is the Reading Terminal Market near the Pennsylvania Convention Center. At this busy marketplace, merchants and farmers sell fresh fruits and vegetables, meat, cheese, and foods from all over the world.

A growing Philadelphia food tradition is The Book and the Cook, one of the largest food festivals in the country. At The Book and the Cook festival, people sample food, listen to talks held by chefs and cookbook writers, and enjoy musical and theatrical performances. All of these events celebrate the good food found in Philadelphia.

is for DELAWARE INDIANS...

The Delaware Indians lived in the Philadelphia area well before European settlers arrived. The Delawares called themselves Lenape or Lenni-Lenape. English settlers later gave them the name Delawares.

The Delawares included several different groups: the Munsee, Unalachtigo, and Unami. The Unami, or Turtle Tribe, lived in the area around Philadelphia in wigwams clustered along the Delaware River. They survived by hunting game and farming maize (Indian corn).

Shortly after William Penn arrived, he be-friended the Delawares. Unlike most English governors of the time, he treated them fairly.

According to some historians, in 1682 the Delawares signed a treaty with Penn in their village, Shackamaxon. The site of this treaty is known today as Penn Treaty Park.

As Europeans continued to settle in the area, the Delawares sold more and more of their land. Thomas Penn, one of William Penn's sons, tricked them out of still more territory. Many Delawares died of smallpox and measles, diseases that Europeans had brought to America. With a dwindling amount of land and the constant danger of attack by other tribes, the Delawares began to move westward. Many eventually settled in what is now Oklahoma.

is for ELFRETH'S ALLEY...

Elfreth's Alley is a narrow cobblestone lane in Center City, tucked neatly between Arch and Race Streets on Second Street. With its small brick houses, white doorways, and busybody mirrors (which let people on the second floor see who is at the front door), the alley provides a charming glimpse into Philadelphia's colonial past. It is the oldest street in the United States where people have lived continuously.

Elfreth's Alley is named for Jeremiah Elfreth, a blacksmith. The street's oldest home, the house at 120-122 Elfreth's Alley, was built in the 1720s. The street's newest homes were built in the early 1800s. During colonial times, families moved in and out quickly. Many of the early residents worked as haberdashers, bakers, printers, carpenters, or artisans. Today, the house at 126 Elfreth's Alley is a museum. Every year on the first weekend in June, the houses on Elfreth's Alley are open to the public for guided tours.

Within walking distance of Elfreth's Alley are many other historical spots. At the Betsy Ross House on Arch Street, visitors can see where the seamstress is said to have sewn the nation's first flag. This typical colonial house also has a cellar kitchen, tiny bedrooms, and model work areas.

The U.S. Mint is another important building near Elfreth's Alley. (The first mint was actually built two blocks from this location.) The Philadelphia Mint is the oldest and largest of the four U.S. Mints. Today the Philadelphia Mint makes money at a lightning-fast pace. It can produce 1.8 million coins every hour!

is for FAIRMOUNT PARK...

Fairmount Park is the largest landscaped city park in the world. In 1876 it was the site of the nation's one hundredth birthday party: the Centennial Exhibition. This huge event brought nearly ten million visitors to Fairmount Park.

With more than nine thousand acres, Fairmount Park remains a beautiful open space today. It has winding creeks, hiking trails, bridle paths, gardens, tennis courts, a zoo, and twenty-nine grand mansions that once belonged to wealthy Philadelphians.

The Schuylkill River divides the park into two sections. The Philadelphia Zoo, a popular stop for children, sits on the west bank. On the east bank is Boathouse Row, home of a collection of rowing clubs known as the Schuylkill Navy.

Boathouse Row makes a very pretty sight at night, with twinkling white lights outlining the buildings along the river.

Another children's favorite in Fairmount Park is Smith Memorial Playground and Playhouse. The playground opened more than one hundred years ago with a carousel and popular giant slide. The playhouse, a three-story building with an old-fashioned town and a foam block room, still delights children today.

At the northern end of Fairmount Park, visitors must leave their cars behind. In this quiet section, hikers can follow nature trails that wind along the Wissahickon Creek among old trees and wildlife.

is for GARDENS...

Philadelphia has a long history of gardening. William Penn imagined the city as a "green country town," with gardens and parks providing a way for people to be close to God. Penn's grandson John created one of the first public gardens in the nation when he planted an English landscape garden on his estate. Another important gardener was John Bartram. In 1730 he planted a botanical garden that grew into one of the most important collections of American plants in the country. Today the John Bartram Association runs Bartram's Garden in West Philadelphia.

Other admired public gardens in Philadelphia include Shofuso (the Japanese House and Garden in Fairmount Park), Pennsylvania Hospital's Physic Garden of eighteenth-century medicinal herbs, the Rose Garden near Independence Hall (which honors the signers of the Declaration of Independence and the U.S. Constitution), and Morris Arboretum of the University of Pennsylvania (which has thousands of rare plants, including many of Philadelphia's oldest trees).

Every year, flower lovers from all over the world come to Philadelphia for the Philadelphia Flower Show, the oldest flower show in the country. At this event, held by the Pennsylvania Horticultural Society, ten acres of indoor space are turned into gardens bursting with colorful flowers. The first show was held in Philadelphia in June 1829. Now the Philadelphia Flower Show takes place every year in early March—a sign to Philadelphians that spring is coming soon.

is for HOSPITALS...

Many historic events in the field of medicine took place in Philadelphia. In 1751 Benjamin Franklin and Dr. Thomas Bond founded the first hospital in the nation: Pennsylvania Hospital. In 1765 Dr. John Morgan started the country's first medical school at the College of Philadelphia (later renamed the University of Pennsylvania). In 1787 the College of Physicians and Surgeons opened, providing a valuable library for health care workers. In 1892 the Wistar Institute of Anatomy and Biology was established. The Wistar Institute is the oldest medical research center in the country.

Philadelphia doctors also played an important role in the treatment of mental illness and surgery.

Dr. Benjamin Rush, who signed the Declaration of Independence, devoted much of his life to mental health care. He became known as the Father of American Psychiatry. Dr. Philip Syng Physick was a master surgeon who invented many tools used in the operating room. He earned the nickname Father of American Surgery.

Philadelphia is still known today for its excellent hospitals and medical schools. People can learn more about the history of health care at Philadelphia's very unusual Mütter Museum. On display there are many odd and interesting objects from medical history, including a tumor from President Grover Cleveland's jawbone!

I is for INDEPENDENCE HALL...

The United States of America was born at Independence Hall. Inside this redbrick building, the Declaration of Independence was signed in 1776, the Articles of Confederation were adopted in 1777, and the U.S. Constitution was drafted and signed in 1787.

When construction of the building began in 1732, the colonists called it the Pennsylvania State House. In 1824 the Marquis de Lafayette (a Frenchman who had fought with the Americans in the Revolutionary War) visited the State House and described it as a "hall of independence." Others echoed his words, and soon the building had a new name. Throughout the years, Independence Hall has been remodeled many times. During the 1850s its basement even served as the city's dog pound!

Today Independence Hall is part of Independence National Historical Park. The park consists of more than forty buildings, including Carpenters' Hall, Congress Hall, Old City Hall, and the new National Constitution Center (a museum that honors the U.S. Constitution).

The Liberty Bell Center is also part of the park. In 1751 the Pennsylvania Assembly ordered the bell to celebrate the fiftieth anniversary of William Penn's Charter of Privileges. (This document later shaped the U.S. Constitution.) In 2003 the bell was moved to its new home in the Liberty Bell Center. Famous for its zigzag-shaped crack, the bell was last rung in February 1846 in honor of George Washington's birthday.

is for JUSTICE...

Under William Penn, Philadelphia's system for punishing criminals was the gentlest in the colonies. As the city expanded, however, conditions for prisoners grew worse. In 1787 a group called the Philadelphia Society for Alleviating the Miseries of Public Prisons met at Benjamin Franklin's house to talk about possible improvements. The Society decided to place prisoners in solitary confinement to see if spending time alone would help them feel sorry about their crimes. This idea of rehabilitating prisoners, or helping them change their ways, was new and different. Soon it was being copied around the world.

Philadelphia's first prison was the Walnut Street Jail on Washington Square, which was built around 1773. For a time, the jail practiced solitary confinement and was believed to treat prisoners well. By the time the jail was torn down in 1835, however, it was overcrowded and conditions were poor.

The Eastern State Penitentiary, which was completed in 1829, was built to keep prisoners in solitary confinement. Eastern State was one of the first prisons to be called a penitentiary, because it was designed to make prisoners feel penitent, or sorry for what they had done. With its large stone walls and turrets, the building looks like a castle. Today the prison is a National Historic Landmark and a museum. Every Halloween it is turned into a very spooky haunted house!

is for
KIMMEL CENTER...

The Kimmel Center for the Performing Arts opened its doors to the public in 2001. Verizon Hall, the center's concert hall, is shaped like a cello. The Perelman Theater, which is used for chamber music, dance, and drama, has an unusual rotating stage. Many visitors admire the building's tall, glass ceiling and state-of-the-art technology.

The Kimmel Center is home to eight of Philadelphia's performing arts groups: the Philadelphia Orchestra, the Opera Company of Philadelphia, the Pennsylvania Ballet, American Theater Arts for Youth, the Philadelphia Chamber Music Society, Peter Nero and the Philadelphia Pops, the Chamber Orchestra of Philadelphia, and the dance company Philadanco.

One block north is the Academy of Music, now part of the Kimmel Center complex. The Academy of Music was first built in the nineteenth century as Philadelphia's opera house. It is a grand building with gold decorations and old-fashioned gaslights at the entrance. Today the Opera Company of Philadelphia, the Pennsylvania Ballet, and musical groups on tour perform at the Academy of Music.

Both the Academy of Music and the Kimmel Center are located along the Avenue of the Arts, the city's entertainment and arts district.

is for LEADERS...

Many Philadelphians stand out as leaders in their fields. Here are some remarkable Philadelphia citizens, from past to present:

Lucretia Coffin Mott (1793–1880) was a Quaker who fought *against* slavery and *for* women's rights. In 1833 Mott founded the Philadelphia Female Anti-slavery Society. In 1848 she helped organize the first women's rights convention in the United States at Seneca Falls, New York.

Maxfield Parrish (1870–1966) was an artist whose illustrations appeared on magazine covers, in ads, and in children's books. Parrish, who grew up in Philadelphia, studied at the Pennsylvania Academy of the Fine Arts. Today his popular artwork can be seen in museums across the United States.

Maggie Kuhn (1905–1995) was forced to retire from her long career at a Philadelphia church at the age of sixty-five. This experience led her to found the Gray Panthers, a group that helps senior citizens. During her lifetime, Kuhn spoke out about discrimination against the elderly and fought for laws to protect their rights.

Dr. José De Celis (1915–1961) was a respected Puerto Rican dentist and community leader. In the 1940s and 1950s, De Celis headed the Latin American Association, a neighborhood group that worked to improve life for Philadelphia's Latino community. He also helped organize Philadelphia's first Puerto Rican Day celebration.

Rev. Leon Sullivan (1922–2001) led the Zion Baptist Church in Philadelphia from 1950 to

1988. In 1977 he established the Sullivan Principles, a code of conduct to guide U.S. companies doing business in South Africa. These principles boldly challenged the South African government's system of apartheid, which segregated black South Africans. In 1992 Sullivan was awarded the Presidential Medal of Freedom, a symbol of great honor in the United States.

Julius Erving (born 1950) played basketball for the Philadelphia 76ers from 1976 to 1987. With his dazzling moves and talent for scoring, "Dr. J" broke records and led the 76ers to a National Basketball Association championship in 1983.

Edward Rendell (born 1944) served as mayor of Philadelphia from 1992 to 1999. He was a popular leader, bringing jobs to the city and improvements to many neighborhoods. In 2003 Rendell became one of only two Philadelphia mayors to be elected governor of Pennsylvania.

is for MUMMERS...

The Mummers are amateur street performers. Mummery began with the first European settlers in the Philadelphia area: Swedish immigrants, who liked to visit friends on December 26, the second day of Christmas. Over time, these visits stretched to New Year's Day, when people gathered in groups to greet the New Year with noisy parades, masquerades, and gunfire. As the groups traveled from house to house, they sang and danced. Before long the bands of entertainers became known as the New Year Shooters and Mummers Association. By the 1870s the celebrations had become a real parade, with Comic Clubs and Fancy Dress Clubs.

Today thousands of people gather to watch Mummers strut down Broad Street on New Year's Day. Four divisions of Mummers perform: Comics (or clowns), Fancies (who wear elaborate costumes), String Bands (the only Mummers with instruments), and Fancy Brigades (groups that perform around a theme). Because the Mummers' routines and colorful costumes require long hours of preparation, family members often pitch in. At City Hall and the Pennsylvania Convention Center, judges award prizes for the best Mummers in each category. People can learn more about this unique Philadelphia tradition at the Philadelphia Mummers Museum in South Philadelphia.

is for

NEIGHBORHOODS...

Many people describe Philadelphia as a collection of different neighborhoods. As the city grew beyond William Penn's original boundaries, neighborhoods began to form. Because people of many different backgrounds settled in Philadelphia, the city has always had a rich mix of ethnic and racial groups. Here are some of Philadelphia's best-known sections and neighborhoods:

Center City (downtown Philadelphia), home of the city's business and financial districts, has many tall skyscrapers. Included among the neighborhoods of Center City are Chinatown, Society Hill, and Olde City. Many popular sites for visitors, such as Independence National Park, City Hall, and the Pennsylvania Convention Center, are located in Center City.

Chestnut Hill, an official Historic District, lies along a cobblestoned section of Germantown Avenue.

The neighborhood has many charming shops and restaurants.

Chinatown, in Center City, is a neighborhood of Chinese-owned restaurants, shops, and homes. Visitors often enter Chinatown through the brightly colored Friendship Gate at Tenth and Arch Streets.

Germantown, home to Philadelphia's first German settlers, is one of the oldest neighborhoods in the city. During the 1800s many Germantown residents became

involved in the anti-slavery movement.

Manayunk, known for its steep hills, sits on the east bank of the Schuylkill River. It is a National Historic neighborhood filled with shops, galleries, and restaurants.

Northeast Philadelphia includes neighborhoods such as Pennypack, Fox Chase, Mayfair, and Oxford Circle. This mostly residential area also has lots of places to shop.

North Philadelphia is a large section of the city where people of many different backgrounds live. It is also the site of Temple University's main campus.

South Philadelphia is the city's sports stadium district. Also found in South Philly are the Italian Market and some of the best cheese steaks around!

University City is part of West Philadelphia. It is the lively area around Drexel University and the University of Pennsylvania.

is for
OUTDOOR
FESTIVALS...

Many outdoor celebrations take place in Philadelphia, including parades for Chinese New Year, St. Patrick's Day, Israel Independence Day, Pulaski Day, Columbus Day, and Thanksgiving. Philadelphia's Odunde Festival, a Nigerian celebration held in honor of Oshun, the goddess of the river, is one of the oldest African American street festivals in the country. Philadelphians celebrate Latino culture at the Penn's Landing Hispanic Fiesta in July and at the Puerto Rican Day parade in September.

Other outdoor events include the Jam on the River (a music festival held in May) and the Rittenhouse Square Fine Arts Annual (a large art show that displays works by more than one hundred local artists). The Welcome America! Festival marks Independence Day with activities that include fireworks, concerts, and a public reading of the Declaration of Independence. At College Day on the Parkway, students can enjoy street performers, arts and crafts, and music and then step inside the museums along the Benjamin Franklin Parkway for free!

is for PHILADELPHIA...

When William Penn designed Philadelphia, he remembered a deadly fire that had spread quickly through London's narrow, crowded streets in 1666. For that reason, Penn laid out Philadelphia in a grid with much wider streets.

Penn made sure to build no walls or barriers around the city so that newcomers would always feel welcome. Philadelphia grew quickly as word of America's beauty and Penn's fair governing style spread. Typical early homes were two-story brick buildings. (Before these homes were built, many of the area's settlers had lived in caves dug out along the Delaware River!)

Soon Philadelphia was the first city of the colonies, with services that were quite unusual for the time, including hospitals, newspapers, a fire company, and streetlights. During the eighteenth century it became a center of politics, manufacturing, and trade. From 1790 to 1800, Philadelphia served as the nation's capital.

In 1871 construction began on City Hall. Located at the intersection of Broad and Market Streets, the 548-foot-high tower is often seen as the heart of the city. City Hall took thirty years to build and is the world's tallest masonry structure without a steel frame. On top of the building is a thirty-seven-foot-tall statue of William Penn created by the famous sculptor Alexander Milne Calder.

Broad Street still runs straight through the city, just as in Penn's original plan. Some of Philadelphia's finest buildings line this grand avenue, including the Pennsylvania Academy of the Fine Arts, the Union League of Philadelphia, the Academy of Music, and the original Girard Trust Company building. Broad Street is the site of many of the city's parades and festivities.

Q *is for* QUAKERS...

In 1681 William Penn received a charter from King Charles II of England to establish a colony in America. Penn based his new colony on a "Holy Experiment" designed to give people freedom of speech and religion and the chance to govern themselves. He named his new city Philadelphia, Greek for "City of Brotherly Love," to show that all people were welcome.

Penn's ideas about government were inspired by the Religious Society of Friends, a group formed in England by the preacher George Fox around 1647. Later a judge called the group Quakers after Fox told him that he must tremble, or quake, at the word of the Lord.

Quaker beliefs were very different from the beliefs of the Church of England. The Church of England held that only members of the clergy could understand God's word. Quakers believe that in every person there is a spark of God. In England many Quakers, including George Fox and William Penn, were jailed for speaking out about these ideas.

Quaker meetinghouses can be found throughout the Philadelphia area. The Arch Street Meeting House in Center City is a typical Quaker place of worship: a plain room with bare floors, simple wooden benches, and no pulpit. On display in the meetinghouse are historical objects, such as Quaker clothing and bibles. The Arch Street Meeting House is the oldest Quaker meetinghouse still in use in Philadelphia and the largest Quaker meetinghouse in the world.

B *is for* RIVERS...

Philadelphia sits between two rivers: the Delaware (to the east) and the Schuylkill (to the west). A third body of water, the Wissahickon Creek, lies to the northwest.

The Delaware River flows for more than three hundred miles from Hancock, New York, to the Delaware Bay. For the Delaware Indians who first lived along its banks and for the Europeans who came later, it was a very important resource. It provided food, water, and a transportation and trading route.

The 125-mile-long Schuylkill River joins the Delaware River in Philadelphia and then empties into the Delaware Bay. The Delaware Indians had two names for the river: Ganshowahanna, which means "falling waters," and Manayunk, which means "where we drink." An explorer from the Dutch East Indies Company later gave the river the name Schuylkill, which means "hidden creek."

It is believed that the Wissahickon Creek was a rich hunting ground for the Delawares, who named it Wissahickon, or "catfish stream." Today the creek winds for about twenty-five miles through towns west of Philadelphia, emptying into a deep gorge as it approaches the city. It joins the Schuylkill River just below City Avenue.

In recent years, environmentalists have worked hard to clean and protect Philadelphia's rivers. Three bronze statues in the fountain at Logan Circle represent the importance of these three waterways to the Philadelphia area.

is for SCULPTURE...

Philadelphia has more outdoor art than any other North American city. The *LOVE* sculpture in John F. Kennedy Plaza, which spells out the word *love* in huge red letters, is one of Philadelphia's best-known pieces. The sculpture playfully recalls William Penn's dream of a City of Brotherly Love. Other favorite public sculptures include Claes Oldenburg's *Clothespin* near City Hall, the Swann Memorial Fountain at Logan Circle, and the *Rocky* statue in front of the Spectrum stadium.

Colorful murals also decorate the city. Since the start of the Mural Arts Program in 1984, more than two thousand paintings have been created throughout Philadelphia's neighborhoods. These include murals of local heroes, such as Patti LaBelle, Mario Lanza, Paul Robeson, and Wilt Chamberlain, and colorful scenes reflecting different neighborhoods. The largest mural in the city is *Common Threads,* at the intersection of Broad and Spring Garden Streets.

Important Philadelphia art museums include the Rodin Museum, which exhibits 124 works by the sculptor Auguste Rodin, and the Philadelphia Museum of Art, the third largest art museum in the country. The Pennsylvania Academy of the Fine Arts, the first art school in the country, displays a wide variety of American art. At the Painted Bride Art Center, visitors can see contemporary art. Works by three generations of the Calder family — Alexander Milne, Alexander Stirling, and Alexander "Sandy"— can be spotted all over town among Philadelphia's many outdoor works of art.

is for TRAINS...

In the nineteenth century, the arrival of steam trains changed life in Philadelphia. The trains provided a new and quicker way of traveling. As tracks were built, connecting Philadelphia to other cities, coal and food could be shipped more easily too.

Philadelphia's Reading Terminal was built in 1892. On the other side of City Hall was the Broad Street Station. About forty small railroads made up the system that later became the Reading Railroad. The Reading Railroad was known for its speedy trains. One especially famous train was the Boardwalk Flyer. It broke records for speed as it hurtled toward Atlantic City, New Jersey.

The last train left Reading Terminal in 1985, and the terminal became a huge marketplace.

Today the three main train stations for the Southeastern Pennsylvania Transit Authority (SEPTA) and Amtrak trains are Market East Station, Thirtieth Street Station, and Penn Center/ Suburban Station. Thirtieth Street Station is an especially grand building, with stone columns, beautiful artwork, and ceilings decorated in gold. When it opened in 1934, it was one of the first major stations for electric trains in the country.

The first elevated subway came to Philadelphia around 1907. Today many Philadelphians use elevated and underground subway trains to travel around the city. The Broad Street line runs north to south along Broad Street. The Market-Frankford line runs east to west along Market Street and then north to south along Frankford Avenue.

is for

UNDERGROUND RAILROAD...

The Underground Railroad was a secret network of stops, or stations, created to help slaves reach freedom in the North. Philadelphia was one of the stops on the Underground Railroad's eastern route. Some Philadelphia stations were the Arch Street Wharf, Reading Railroad Terminal, Paschall's Alley, Mother Bethel African Methodist Episcopal Church, the First Congregational Unitarian Church, and private homes such as the Johnson House in Germantown. From Philadelphia, slaves were transported farther north by train, by boat, or by foot.

Three men who helped run the city's Underground Railroad were James Forten, Robert Purvis, and William Still. Many other Philadelphians risked their lives by hiding runaway slaves in their homes and businesses. Henrietta Bowers Duterte, an African American woman who was the first female undertaker in Philadelphia, even helped slaves by hiding them in caskets!

Philadelphia's location and large community of supporters made it a very important stop on the Underground Railroad. It is believed that by 1860 about nine thousand fugitive slaves had passed through the city's Underground Railroad stations.

V is for VALLEY FORGE...

In 1777, during the Revolutionary War, British forces captured Philadelphia. General George Washington planned a surprise attack to drive out the British troops, but the plan failed. With no choice but to wait out the cold winter, Washington marched his army to Valley Forge on the west side of the Schuylkill River.

Conditions in the camp at Valley Forge were terrible. Poor roads and bad weather made it almost impossible to get supplies. The soldiers often went hungry, and many suffered through the winter with no coats or shoes. Thousands lost their lives to disease.

Still the story of Valley Forge is not all bleak. By spring, the roads had improved and supplies began to arrive steadily. Fish filled the Schuylkill River. France sent word that it would enter the war as an ally of the colonies. Washington had also proved his talent as a leader. Despite the grim conditions, he had managed to train and unify his army. By the time Washington's men left Valley Forge, they had gained the skills—and the hope—they needed to defeat the British.

Today Valley Forge is a National Historical Park. Visitors can explore the site where Washington and his ragged army camped during that long, harsh winter.

is for

WASHINGTON SQUARE...

William Penn's design for Philadelphia included five city parks. These parks, which started as patches of forest, did not become true city squares until the nineteenth century. Today four remain: Washington Square, Franklin Square, Rittenhouse Square, and Logan Circle. In 1871 the fifth square, Center Square, became the site of City Hall.

Each square has its own special history. During the eighteenth century, Washington Square, named for George Washington, served as a potter's field (a burial ground for poor people) and a cemetery for Revolutionary War soldiers. Today it is the site of the Tomb of the Unknown Soldier, which honors Washington and the Revolutionary War soldiers who died for this nation's freedom.

Franklin Square, named for Benjamin Franklin, was used to store ammunition during the Revolutionary War. It was also a colonial burial ground and the site of cattle and horse markets. Today the square has a playground, a baseball diamond, and a pool.

Rittenhouse Square, named for colonial scholar David Rittenhouse, is the only Philadelphia square that was never used as a burial ground. At one time, it served as a pasture for cows, pigs, and chickens, but today it is an elegant city park with a playground and beautiful sculptures.

Logan Circle was named for James Logan, who was once secretary to William Penn and a mayor of Philadelphia. First designed as a square park, it was reshaped as a circle when the Benjamin Franklin Parkway was built. In the middle of Logan Circle is the Swann Memorial Fountain, the site of some of the finest public sculptures in the nation.

X is for XYLOPHONES...

Philadelphia's long history as a musical center dates back to colonial times. In 1703 a group of long-haired men called the Hermits of the Wissahickon held the first public concert in the area. By 1728 choral groups were growing rapidly and a pipe organ had been installed in Christ Church.

Philadelphia's Curtis Institute of Music was founded in 1924. It was the first tuition-free music conservatory in the country. Many of the gifted musicians trained by the Curtis Institute have gone on to perform in well-known orchestras.

During the 1940s and 1950s, Philadelphia "crooners" Eddie Fisher and Al Martino sang their way to national success. Meanwhile, in the 1950s, *American Bandstand* began broadcasting from a Philadelphia television studio. Hosted by Dick Clark, this live dance show became a huge hit, especially among teenagers.

In the 1970s, Kenneth Gamble and Leon Huff created a new sound. Their recordings of Harold Melvin and the Blue Notes, Billy Paul, and other soulful Philadelphia artists came to be known as the Sound of Philadelphia.

The founding of the Philadelphia Orchestra in 1900 was another important event in Philadelphia's musical history. Under Leopold Stokowski (who conducted from 1912 to 1936) and Eugene Ormandy (who conducted from 1936 to 1980), the orchestra became known around the world.

For many years the Philadelphia Orchestra played at the Academy of Music. Now its home is Verizon Hall at the Kimmel Center for the Performing Arts. Thanks to Verizon Hall's state-of-the-art sound system, concerts have certainly come a long way from the first public performance by the Hermits of the Wissahickon!

is for YOUTH...

Many of the nation's earliest schools were founded in Philadelphia. In 1684 a man named Enoch Flower started a school for children, charging fees based on what he taught. (Parents paid four shillings for their children to learn reading and six shillings for them to learn reading *and* writing.) In 1689 the Society of Friends created the William Penn Charter School, the first school to educate poor children for free. This was the start of public education in America. Founded in 1759, Germantown Academy is the oldest school in the nation that is not connected with a religious group. Penn Charter and Germantown Academy are both still open today.

Some of the country's first universities began in Philadelphia too. The University of Pennsylvania was the first university in the country that was not built for a particular religious group. It was founded in 1749 by Benjamin Franklin, who believed that college should prepare students for careers in business and public service as well as religion. The nation's first art school for women, the Philadelphia School of Design for Women, opened its doors in 1848. Later it was renamed the Moore College of Art and Design. Today it is one of only two art and design colleges for women in the world.

A true college town, Philadelphia is home to more than twenty-five colleges and universities. Many more lie just outside Philadelphia's borders. Some of the city's best-known schools are the University of Pennsylvania, Temple University, Drexel University, La Salle University, the Curtis Institute of Music, and the University of the Arts.

Z is for ZOO...

The Philadelphia Zoo was the first zoo in the nation. It opened its gates in Fairmount Park on July 1, 1874. On that first day, visitors could see 282 animals, including 43 species of American mammals and animals from Australia and Asia. Instead of the zoo monorail that transports people today, goat carts carried the first zoo visitors!

In 1875 a male Indian rhinoceros named Pete was added to the collection. He was the first rhinoceros ever seen at an American zoo. Other famous residents have included a female Indian rhinoceros named Peggy, a six-ton elephant named Bolivar, and a fifty-five-year-old gorilla named Massa.

Today the zoo has more than sixteen hundred rare and exotic animals from around the world, along with forty-two acres of gardens. Popular stops include the Reptile and Amphibian House, Bear Country, Bird Valley, the African Plains, and the Primate Reserve. The Zooballoon, a hot-air balloon ride, lifts visitors four hundred feet above Fairmount Park. The Children's Zoo, also the first in the country, has duck and turtle ponds, a petting yard, a Bunny Village, and a theater with live animal shows.

The Philadelphia Zoo is known around the world for its research in animal diseases and behavior. Today it continues its strong mission of conservation, education, research, and recreation.

ILLUSTRATION CREDITS

(in order of appearance)

Amanda Montalvo, Woodrow Wilson Middle School

Khoanh Lung Ung, Olney Elementary School

Julian Gantt, C. W. Henry Elementary School

Zakarya Banks, Hill-Freedman Middle School

Talani Mathis, J. R. Masterman Middle School

Elie Berman-Brodsky, C. W. Henry Elementary School

Leigh Jenkins, George Sharswood School

Nathan McHugh, MYA (Middle Years Alternative School for the Humanities)

Margaret Bateman, C. W. Henry Elementary School

Chris Balionis, George Sharswood School

Kenneth Casper, George Sharswood School

Kurtis Fisher, W. T. Tilden Middle School

Marat Kanafin, Woodrow Wilson Middle School

Charona R. Jackson, W. T. Tilden Middle School

Georgiy Khokhlov, Albert M. Greenfield School

Shakira Yancy, Bache-Martin School

Naomy Valenti-Cromartie, Russell Conwell Middle School

Jasmine Anderson, C. E. Pickett Middle School

Gokul Kumar, William H. Loesche Elementary School

Charifa David, MYA (Middle Years Alternative School for the Humanities)

Jonathan Baez, J. H. Webster School

Darla Clark-Martin, J. R. Masterman Middle School

Leah Mitchell, W. T. Tilden Middle School

Kiesha Evans, Hill-Freedman Middle School

Grace Lam, D. N. Fell School

Devont Miller, Samuel Gompers School

Keyna McClinek, Hill-Freedman Middle School

Cynthia King, Ethel Allen School

ABOUT THE AUTHOR

Susan Korman is the author of over twenty books for young readers, including titles in the Smithsonian Institution Backyard series, *Groundhog at Evergreen Road* and *Box Turtle at Silver Pond Lane*; biographies of Sammy Sosa and Sir Walter Raleigh; and middle-grade fiction in series such as the Magic Attic Club, Ghostwriter, and Silver Blades. Formerly a children's book editor, she currently works as a freelance writer and is studying to become a school librarian. She lives in Yardley, Pennsylvania, with her husband and three children.

EXECUTIVE EDITOR
Micah Kleit

AUTHOR
Susan Korman

INSTITUTIONAL COLLABORATION
School District of Philadelphia
Office of Creative and Performing Arts
   Dennis W. Creedon, EdD, *Administrator*
   Tessie Varthas, *Lead Academic Coach/Art Education*
City of Philadelphia
Office of the Mayor
Philadelphia Reads
   Thomas S. Jacoby, *Executive Director*

MANUSCRIPT EDITOR
Joan Polsky Vidal

DEVELOPMENT
Temple University
Office of Development & Alumni Affairs
   Brooke Cho, *Director of Development, Temple University Press*
   Meredith Keiser, *Director of Corporate Relations*

PUBLISHER
Alex Holzman

DESIGN
Andrea Hemmann/GHI Design

ALPHABET ILLUSTRATION
Gina Triplett

PRODUCTION DIRECTOR
Charles H. E. Ault

PRODUCTION ASSISTANCE
Jennifer French

COMPOSITION
GHI Design

PRINTING
Friesens Printers

This book was composed in Mrs. Eaves and Centennial typefaces and was printed on 100# Luna Matte paper.